D1202534

Cover Design: Christoper Thomas of Chris Thomas Graphics
Interior Design: Brandi K. Etheredge
Copy Editor: Yvette R. Blair-Lavallais

BLUEPRINT FOR BIBLE Basics

BY ALEX McELROY

FOREWORD BY JOHN HANNAH

DEDICATION

Nothing is possible, including life itself, without God. Our relationship with Him would not be possible without His Son Jesus Christ. Therefore, I give all the honor, praise and glory to Him. I am so grateful for this and every blessing that He has bestowed upon me.

First, I'd like to thank my wife who is truly a part of me forever! I'd like to dedicate this to my daughters, Michaela and Grace, who make me want to be a better man everyday.

I'd like to thank Pastor Hannah for being my Pastor and leader. I thank God for my divinely-connected, big brother, Pastor Tim. I also praise God for my spiritual brothers, Pastor Nick, Matt and Destry. I love you all and I love my Identity family.

I also praise God for my mother, brother, and sister-in-law.

I'd like to give a special thanks to Rev. Russell St. Bernard and Rev. Yvette R. Blair for stepping in at the right time to make this book happen!

Lastly, I dedicate this to the Kingdom of God that will be impacted for generations to come.

God bless!

FOREWORD

In doing Youth Ministry for years I really didn't know where to start. This led me to begin with the Gospel according to John, which is the gospel to all nations. However, there is so much more knowledge about God and His Word that needs to be communicated. Alex has provided us with a Blueprint to make sure that our youth get a strong foundation. If every youth pastor and every youth took this blueprint and literally built a foundation, that alone would ensure that their years are solid. Anything that they build on this blueprint won't be built on sinking sand but rather it will be built on a secure foundation. This book is a step-by-step guide to guarantee that we are laying a sound underpinning in order to make certain these young people become everything that God has called them to be. I know for a fact there are people who have been in church all their lives but still don't know the basics of salvation, how to lead their peers to the Lord, and may not even be certain of their own salvation.

This Blueprint will give our youth all the necessary tools that they need to make sure that they don't remain in church for years without any substantive growth. This will also assure that they can share the gospel of Jesus Christ with their peers. In 1 Corinthians 9:22 Paul said, "To the weak I became weak, to win the weak. I have become all things to all people so that by all possible means I might save some." We need to be confident that we're building up young people who can share the gospel on that level so that they can save some. This blueprint is definitely the tool to use, not just for youth but for youth leaders. As we empower people and put people in position to lead our youth we need to provide that they have a tool like this book in their hands that will enable them to give our kids the foundation they need in order to live a successful Christian life.

Alex came to New Life Covenant Church and has been part of our leadership now for 10 years. I've seen him start out working with Identity, our teen youth ministry and literally be put in a position with a demand placed on him to teach young people the Word of God and succeed. We put him in a room with some teenagers and saw lives changed! This was because he gave them the basic tools that were needed. And the same young people that we saw Alex in the room with 10 years ago are still an active and intricate part of the ministry today and have grown in their knowledge of the Word. This lets me know that their foundation is solid. He is a family man and he is devoted to his wife and daughters and truly desires to see young people learn their place in the Kingdom of God and to then make an impact within the Kingdom of God. As you read and teach this blueprint to our youth rest assured that these lessons are the building blocks to creating strong leaders and young men and women who are Kingdom-minded!

Pastor John F. Hannah
New Life Covenant Southeast

TABLE OF CONTENTS

PLAN OF SALVATION

"Nothing can compare with all that is ours in Christ when we find salvation. Forgiveness. Justification. Adoption. Eternal life. What a glorious life the Gospel offers to those who are searching for purpose and meaning or to those who have found that materialism and sensual pleasure are not the answer to the deepest yearnings of the heart. The crowning glory of salvation is promised when we enter into the presence of the King. We have a home in heaven reserved for us and awards that await us. No wonder the Gospel is "Good News." Unfortunately, many people today have distorted the meaning of salvation."
- Evangelist Billy Graham

The PLEA for SALVATION

If the key to eternal life was just behind a door, what would you do to gain access to that door? What would you give up to get past it? Most of us would probably give whatever it took to get through it. Eternal life and access to God is much more attainable than trying to break through a locked door. Our access is through salvation in Jesus Christ. Salvation is freedom from the eternal effects of the sins that we have committed. The freedom is possible because of the death of Jesus on the Cross and His resurrection. The eternal punishment for sin is eternal death or permanent separation from God. The price was paid for us: Jesus gave his life and

He **willingly** paid it. The Bible lays out the plan of salvation in the book of Romans, written by Paul and found in the New Testament. It starts with why we need salvation in Romans 1:18-32, then explains how we can obtain salvation, how God provides us access to salvation, and finally, the benefits that we receive once we have salvation. Romans 3:23-24 says, "For all have sinned and fall short of the glory of God, being justified freely by His grace through the redemption that is in Christ Jesus." We have all sinned, so there is no one above any other. Sin can be explained as "missing the mark." It would be falling short of the standard set by God, which is holiness. Holiness is perfection. Holiness is the perfect character or nature of God. It is purity of the highest level.

The PLAN for SALVATION

Once sin entered the world (read Genesis 3), God knew this standard would be impossible for us to meet. But He had a permanent solution in mind before we even knew we needed one! Romans 2:11 lets us know that there is no partiality in God. Since we have all sinned, no one can hold anyone more accountable than the other. In God's eyes, sin is sin and we all need forgiveness. The goal has been clearly established that His glory (His essence) is what we should be seeking. We are incapable or unable to obtain it on our own. We always miss the mark. God, in his holiness can't look upon sin, so there has to be some way to get sin off of us before we can even approach God. Think of sin as being permanently dirty, to the point that no amount of showers could cleanse you. The only cleansing agent capable of cleansing you of sin from the inside out is the blood of Jesus. When you get a bad cut that happens sometimes while you are playing basketball there is often a scar that remains after the cut stops bleeding. That permanent scar is like sin and a Holy God can't look on sin. However, your faith in Jesus allows His blood to cover up that scar so that God sees you as He sees His own Son. Therefore, the solution is faith in Jesus Christ. Christ justified us (acquitted or found not guilty and declared us righteous). Romans 6:23 says "For the wages of sin is death but the gift of God is eternal life in Christ Jesus our Lord." We deserve death because of the sin of Adam and Eve in the Garden of Eden, but God freely gives us eternal life through our faith in the power of the blood of His Son Jesus that was shed on the cross.

Consider the following example to help understand this concept of what takes place when we sin. When you go to the store and buy some shoes, you decide what those shoes are worth to you, or their value. If the shoes cost $100, you will pay $100 for them because you believe that having those shoes is more valuable to you than having the $100. Likewise, when you sin you are, in essence, saying this sin is more valuable to you at this moment than your fellowship with God. And you trade your sin for a piece of fellowship with God. Once that transaction is made, there are no refunds. The wages of sin is death; however, Jesus paid those wages for you! The *gift* of God is eternal life; this is yours, once you have accepted Jesus as your Lord and Savior.

The PRIZE of SALVATION

Romans 10:9-10 says "If you confess with your mouth the Lord Jesus and believe in your heart that God has raised Him from the dead you will be saved. For with the heart, one believes unto righteousness and with the mouth confession is made unto salvation." You must confess with your mouth, and only you can do that. Going to church does not get you into heaven. Belief in God does not even get you into heaven. James 2:19 tells us that even the demons believe in God and tremble. The difference between believing in God and confessing Christ as your Savior is that confessing Jesus as Lord recognizes His perfect life lived on earth, His sacrifice of being beaten and nailed to a cross and left there to die, being laid in a tomb for 3 days, conquering satan and the grave and being raised again to life! That confession gives you salvation. It cannot be earned and we do not deserve it. It is something given to you through belief in and recognition of Christ's suffering on the cross. Your faith in Christ and His plan of salvation is assurance of His love for all of us.

STUDY GUIDE

MEMORIZE: ROMANS 10:9 (NKJV)
..."that if you confess with your mouth the Lord Jesus and believe in your heart that God has raised Him from the dead, you will be saved."

Re-read the opening quote at the beginning of this chapter. Dissect the quote: What does salvation mean to you and what are some of the benefits of being saved?

SHORT ANSWER
Directions: Answer each of the following questions in at least TWO COMPLETE sentences. The answers come from your lesson.

1. How did God give us the gift of eternal life?

2. What is a wage? What is the wage of sin?

3. Explain this statement : "Sin costs you something, but salvation is a gift."

4. What are some of your thoughts on what is lost in a moment of sin?

5. What gives us access to God and heaven? Why is this access important?

6. What proof do we have that God defeated death?

ESSAY QUESTION

Directions: Answer the following essay question in at least two well-thought out paragraphs. Use at least three specific scriptures to support your essay.

Question: Look back over your life and think of any sins that you've committed that you need to be forgiven for and have already been forgiven (refer to Romans 1:26-32) and describe how God's plan of salvation can be applied to your life. Remember, no matter what you have done in the past, God loves you!

LIFE APPLICATION:
Simple proof test if challenged on the truth of the resurrection.

Pretend for a moment that I am Jesus and that you are one of my disciples. For three and a half years you are with me and you hear me preach about my Kingdom and what it entails. You also hear me tell you that I am going to die a gruesome death and be buried and that after three days I'm going to get up and walk out of the grave. Now, because of the amazing things you've seen me do and the miracles you've seen me perform, you accept this crazy prediction. However, once I'm crucified and– if I don't get up and walk out of the grave, are you going to continue to believe that I am the Son of God and that everything I said was true? In other words, if I stay dead would you still call yourself my follower and preach in my name and plant churches in my name especially when your own life is in jeopardy of death just for being connected to me?

Other person: No. I would say, "I guess he was a liar" and go on about my business.

Response: Exactly. Therefore, the very fact that the disciples didn't do that and that they did preach the message of Jesus and that they did plant churches and that they did write the gospels and the rest of the New Testament and that they were willing to die gruesome deaths proves that Jesus was raised from the grave and resurrected (brought back to life) by God, because if He had not been, the movement He started would have died with Him. The fact that the New Testament even exists is proof that its words are true.

Would you give your life for a liar?

This is how some of the early apostles died:

MATTHEW
Suffered martyrdom in Ethiopia, killed by a sword wound.

MARK
Died in Alexandria, Egypt after being dragged by horses through the streets.

LUKE
Was hanged in Greece as a result of his tremendous preaching to the lost.

JOHN
Faced martyrdom when he was boiled in a huge basin of boiling oil during a wave of persecution in Rome. However, he was miraculously delivered from death. John was then sentenced to the mines on the prison Island of Patmos to live in exile where he wrote his prophetic Book of Revelation. John was later freed and returned to serve as Bishop of Edessa in modern Turkey. He died as an old man, and was the only apostle to die peacefully.

PETER
Was crucified upside down on an x-shaped cross. According to church tradition, it was because he told his tormentors that he felt unworthy to die in the same way that Jesus Christ had died.

JAMES
The leader of the church in Jerusalem, was thrown over a hundred feet down from the southeast pinnacle of the Temple when he refused to deny his faith in Christ. When they discovered that he survived the fall, his enemies beat James to death with a fuller's club.

JAMES THE GREAT
Son of Zebedee, was a fisherman by trade when Jesus called him to a lifetime of ministry. As a strong leader of the church, James was ultimately beheaded at Jerusalem. The Roman officer who guarded James watched amazed as James defended his faith at his trial. Later, the officer walked beside James to the place of execution. Overcome by conviction, he declared his new faith to the judge and knelt beside James to accept beheading as a Christian.

BARTHOLOMEW
Also known as Nathaniel, he was a missionary to Asia. He witnessed for our Lord in present day Turkey. Bartholomew was martyred for his preaching in Armenia where he was flayed to death by a whip.

ANDREW
Was crucified on an x-shaped cross in Patras, Greece. After being whipped severely by seven soldiers, his body was tied to the cross

with cords to prolong his agony. His followers reported that, when he was led toward the cross, Andrew saluted it in these words: 'I have long desired and expected this happy hour. The cross has been consecrated by the body of Christ hanging on it'. He continued to preach to his tormentors for two days until he died.

THOMAS
Was stabbed with a spear while in India during one of his missionary trips to establish the church in the Sub-continent.

JUDE
Was killed with arrows when he refused to deny his faith in Christ.

MATTHIAS
The apostle chosen to replace the traitor Judas Iscariot, was stoned and then beheaded.

PAUL
Was tortured and then beheaded by the evil Emperor Nero at Rome in A.D. 67. Paul endured a lengthy imprisonment, which allowed him to write some of his many epistles to the churches he had formed throughout the Roman Empire.

WORSHIPPING THE WORTHY

"Praise and worship is powerful, and oh so wonderful! The power in praise and worship goes beyond what you could imagine! Praise and Worship is one of the keys to coming to know Jesus better. Yet some don't understand praise and worship or the true purpose of it. So I thought I would take the time to explain what praise and worship really is and the power behind praise and worship when done right. There cannot be true worship without praise, praise produces worship. Praise means to speak well of God, praise is to acknowledge what God has done. Praise invokes God's presence. It gets God's attention, it creates an atmosphere. Praise is to the New Testament what sacrifices and offering was to the Old Testament, praise is sacrifice. **Psalm 22:3** says that God inhabits the praises of His people, so when God's people praise Him, He draws near and worship results. God has given each of us a **praise** ministry with a **worship** "team" that is never any farther away than an inch below our nose: our lips, mouth, and tongue." - Terrance Williams

WHO we WORSHIP

Let's begin with a very simple concept. Everyone worships something or someone whether they want to admit it or not. Think about it. Some people worship money, education, power, themselves, musicians, world leaders, fame, cars, drugs, other gods, their knowledge, or even the devil. Worship is adoration, devotion and respect usually to a deity. It means to love someone or something so deeply that you revere them or it. *We* are created to worship God. He deserves our worship. You praise God for what He does or has done but you worship Him for who He is. Even as you are reading this, the angels in heaven are singing "Holy, Holy, Holy" as the apostle John shares in Revelation 4:8. God is our creator and everything we do should in some way give Him glory. He is the source of everything. Colossians 1:15-17 reveals that nothing exists or can exist without Him or outside of Him. It is a given that we should worship God because without Him, we would have nothing. God is the great *I Am* who met Moses on the mountain. God is the creator of the universe and He is omnipotent (unlimited power, able to do anything). While humanity is made in God's image, we are not at God's level of holiness and perfection.

Many people worship many things. Unfortunately, anyone or anything receiving our worship outside of our Father God is unworthy of that honor. People worship musicians but those musicians didn't create you and can't save you. In other words why would we worship someone who is equal to us or on our level? People worship money, but that money can only buy you things that could be lost or taken. The things that you do hold on to can't be taken with you when you die. Ecclesiastes 5:15 tells us, "As he came from his mother's womb, naked shall he return, To go as he came; And he shall take nothing from his labor, Which he may carry away in his hand."

Some people worship prestige and accolades that they receive but they don't realize that it was God that allowed them to reach those achievements or to be in the position to receive such high approval. Think about it like this: everything has a beginning, *except* God, which means everything also has an end. We were not created to waste our worship on things that are not eternal, and therefore, we should not do so. (2 Cor. 4:18.) This would be pointless because none of those things can give us eternal life. Instead, we need to offer our worship to *the* eternal source of power, life, and glory – our God in heaven. If we give our devotion to things that can be broken, misplaced, stolen, lost, damaged or devalued then we are bestowing an honor on those things that should be reserved for something that will never and can never be lost or devalued such as an eternal God. Likewise, when we worship people who can disappoint us, mistreat us, lie to us, confuse us, abuse us, stop loving us and eventually die, then we grant them a place in our heart that they should never own and that they can never fulfill. Only a perfect, loving, and eternal God should be given such a great honor as to receive our worship and our reverence.

WAYS we WORSHIP

There are times we sing to worship and there are times where we simply speak well of Him. It doesn't matter where we are: at church, home, in the car, at school – the bottom line is we need to worship Him. If you can't sing well, sing anyway! Singing to the Lord gives Him the glory He deserves and He doesn't care how you sound. Singing is not the only way to worship. Dancing, rapping, playing an instrument and praying are all ways to cry out to Him.

The most important way to worship Him is through our lifestyle - how we live our life as men and women of God. Psalm 102:18 says, "before you were even born God had a plan to create a worshipper like you." Romans 12:1-2 says "I beseech you therefore, brethren, by the mercies of God, that you present your bodies as a living sacrifice, holy, acceptable to God, which is your reasonable service. And do not be conformed to this world but be transformed by the renewing of your mind, that you may prove what is that good and acceptable and perfect will of God." His good, pleasing and perfect will is the safest place to be. When you live a life that is devoted to Him, that is worship. This means that how you speak and conduct yourself needs to represent the Holy God that you serve. When your peers are cursing, you don't. When they are having sex, you don't. When they are drinking or smoking or doing anything that you know Jesus didn't do and would not approve of, you don't! You don't refrain from these things simply because you know they're wrong; rather, you refrain from them because you know *why* they're wrong—they separate you from God. In other words it's not just important that you don't do these things, but the reason why is more important. You choose not to do them because you love Jesus *so* much that you don't want to risk offending Him and what He did for you on the cross.

Psalm 119:126-128 says, "It is time for You to act, O LORD, For they have regarded Your law as void. Therefore I love Your commandments, More than gold, yes, than fine gold! Therefore all Your precepts concerning all things I consider to be right; I hate every false way." This is *true* worship. It isn't forced. It comes from a place of understanding the Word of God and having a relationship with the God *of* the Word. When the Bible becomes reality to us we will be able to worship God in spirit and in truth. (John 4:23-24).

STUDY GUIDE

MEMORIZE: JOHN 4:23 (NKJV)
"But the hour is coming, and now is, when the true worshipers will worship the Father in spirit and truth; for the Father is seeking such to worship Him."

Re-read the opening quote at the beginning of this chapter. Dissect the quote: Why is God worthy of your worship and how do you worship Him?

SHORT ANSWER
Directions: Answer each of the following questions in at least TWO COMPLETE sentences. The answers come from your lesson.

1. What are 2 different ways to worship?

2. What role does lifestyle play in worship?

3. What are some things people worship instead of God?

LIFE APPLICATION:
Action Step 1
This week find a Christian artist who fits your genre style (contemporary,

rap, traditional choir, praise and worship, etc.) and spend at least 15-20 minutes a day listening and worshiping this week.

Action Step 2
Read the lyrics of the music you are listening to. All of your music does not necessarily need to be Christian music, but listen to artists that will impact your life and most importantly not hinder you from bringing glory to God.

Action 3
Come out of your comfort zone this week at church. Worship God in a way that will bring glory to Jesus. (For example, you could bow to your knees, dance, or lay prostrate.)

TESTIMONIAL:
Sometimes when you are worshipping you may cry. Don't feel like you are a punk. I was a tough guy but I have never cried so much in my life as I did when God began to work on me. The reason you cry is that sometimes your flesh can't handle where your spirit is going; therefore, its only response is to break down and cry. Don't fight it. That's the process God uses to get you to be more like Him – who He created you to be.

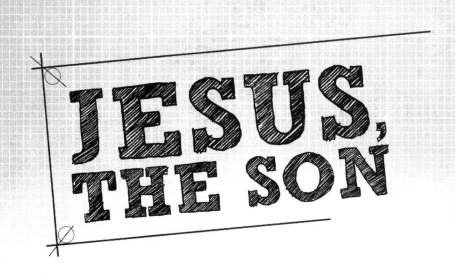

JESUS, THE SON

"You can't lead the people if you don't love the people. You can't save the people if you don't serve the people...Jesus is and was the ultimate leader and servant."
– Cornel West

JESUS, our SUPPORTER

Order, order, order court is now in session. Jesus is the true Son of God. 1 John 2:1 describes Jesus the Lord as our advocate. If we picture this as something like a courtroom trial we would be the defendant. The adversary, (the devil) would be the prosecutor (Revelations 12:10) and Jesus would be our defense attorney or advocate. God the Father is the judge (Romans 2:2). The devil constantly goes before the throne of God to accuse you of the sins that you have committed. If you are not saved and covered by the blood of Jesus then those charges may stand. However, if you are saved through your confession in Jesus Christ your sins have been imputed (attributed or credited) to Jesus. This means you have been justified or declared 'not guilty' – permanently! This is because, in essence, Jesus took your place on the witness stand. You were guilty of lying, cheating, stealing, lusting, or cursing but Jesus said I'll take the punishment for that. The only thing He asks in return is that you don't make His sacrifice worthless. Every time you declare Jesus as your Savior and teach someone else why they should do the same you make certain that the blood that Jesus shed on the cross was not in vain but was in fact a worthy and worthwhile sacrifice.

This is a great scenario for any believer. We are related to the judge as His child and the defense attorney (the judge's Son) is our brother as well (Romans 8:29). In Jesus, we have the best advocate we could possibly hope for. He was at all points tempted (Hebrews 4:15) just as we are which means He can identify with us! We often think that since Jesus was fully God and fully human that He had some kind of special power not to sin or to not give in to temptation or sin but that's not the case. He was fully capable *of* sinning but chose not to because He had you and me on His mind and He knew that if He sinned He would prevent us from having salvation, direct access to God and potentially a place in heaven (2 Cor. 5:21).

JESUS, our SAVIOR

If you have the Son, who is Jesus Christ, you have life (1 John 5:12). Let's examine why we need a savior in the first place. Sin entered the earth (read Genesis 3), which made the Savior necessary. Did you know Jesus was present in Genesis? You can find Jesus in every book of the Bible in some form or fashion. In Genesis 3:15, He's referred to as the *Seed* that would come. The Seed, with a capital letter "S", represents Jesus Christ: the Messiah, the coming one, the Savior. God knew that at a certain point in time (Gal. 4:4), it would be necessary to send Jesus, His Son, in human form to enter the world. The plan was for Jesus to defeat satan by coming to earth and then having lived and died in this realm as a perfect sacrifice, He went to hell and defeated satan once and for all. He took back the keys of life and through His own sacrifice, gave us access to eternal life (Rev. 1:18). Jesus shed His blood on the cross, and because He was a sinless man, that was the last sacrifice necessary. Before this, though, the Jews were required to sacrifice different animals to God in order to atone for their sins. However, when Jesus shed *His* blood, the fact that it came from a sinless man was enough to appease God the Father forever! No more sacrifice needed to be offered and none more perfect could ever be offered that would supersede Christ's death on the cross (Hebrews 9:19-28).

The best news is yet to come. Jesus didn't stay dead! He rose again after three days, having conquered death and satan. Had He not risen and come back to life, His sacrifice would have been in vain and you and I would still be looking for a Savior. If Jesus was still dead and had not been resurrected that would make Him just another man and no more worthy of our faith than anyone else. He would, in turn, be unable to save us from the penalty of our sins. Also, if He had sinned, that would have made His death null and void as well because He wouldn't be any different than us. This is why some religions and some people want to deny the fact of His resurrection. However, there were witnesses who saw and testified to the fact that He *did* die, and He *did* come back to life and walked around before ascending into heaven (Acts 1:9-10). 1 Cor. 15:4-7 says, "and that He was buried, and that He rose again the third day according to the Scriptures, and that He was seen by Cephas, then by the twelve. After that He was seen by over five hundred brethren at once, of whom the greater part remain to the present, but some have fallen asleep. After that He was seen by James, then by all the apostles."

It is important for every believer to be *certain* in their hearts of the truth of the resurrection. Without the resurrection, as the apostle Paul goes onto say, "if Christ is not risen, then our preaching *is* empty and your faith *is* also empty (1 Cor. 15:14). Think about the following as well, if you are ever challenged on this fact. When Jesus was led away to be crucified, the Roman government conducted a community-wide search for Christians (followers of Christ or followers of 'the way') who were showing allegiance to Christ and not to the Emperor. This meant that anyone who was preaching or teaching in the name of Jesus would have to do so at the risk of death. Jesus told all of the disciples that He would die and come back to life after three days. They had seen Him do some amazing things so they were inclined to believe Him. If, as some claim, He didn't die and come back to life from the grave after three days why would the disciples risk preaching about Him, and planting churches in His name and writing extensive letters about Him and His message if He was in essence a liar who was still dead? The answer is, they wouldn't! No rational human being would proclaim the message of a liar who claimed to be the Son of God and died like every other man. The very fact that they wrote about Him and proclaimed His message about the Kingdom that He established on earth and were willing to die horrible deaths for His sake in and of itself *proves* that everything He said was in fact true. The existence of the New Testament is verification that they were certain that they had seen, touched and spoken to the *risen* Christ.

JESUS, our STANDARD

Jesus Christ is not His first and last name. Both names are representative of His function. When God placed Jesus in Mary by the power of the Holy Spirit, He sent an angel to Joseph (Jesus' earthly father) to let him know what to name the baby and why. The Holy Spirit did not sleep with Mary. This was a supernatural conception. The angel said to name Him 'Jesus' which means "the Lord shall save" (Matt. 1:21). Christ means "The Anointed One" (Luke 9:20, John 6:69). The name of Jesus Christ is so important because His name is representative of His function. When we confess (speak) that name and declare Him as our personal Lord and Savior, we acknowledge His position as God's Son, a perfect man, and our intermediary (middle man) between us and God. Philippians 2:9-11 dictates the power of His name.

In order to understand why the life, ministry, death and resurrection of Jesus is so important, we need to remember that Jesus is fully God and fully man. He is one hundred percent God and one hundred percent man. The reason that He couldn't skip over earth and go straight from heaven to hell to defeat satan is because that would make it impossible for us to model His life on earth. He had to live a perfect, sinless life on earth. He faced and avoided temptation here on earth to show us that life without sin was difficult but possible. However, since He knew that we would fall short despite our best efforts He *chose* to die by being nailed to the cross on Mount Calvary. At the moment of His death on the cross, He took the sins of the world (past, present and future) upon Himself. If we believe in Him and confess Him as our Savior, we will have our sins washed away (Psalm 103:12) permanently.

Some people or groups want to discount the importance and the truth of who Jesus was as the Son of God and His life as the Messiah (Savior) on earth. However, they fail to realize that a perfect and holy God can only be accessed by another holy person. This is why we pray to God 'in Jesus' name. *Only* Jesus gives us access to God and ultimately to heaven (John 14:6). This is why it is *so* important to personally understand the role Jesus played. He provided a method of salvation, paid a price for which we could never save up enough to be able to pay, and now He helps us to love like He loves and to draw others to Him through our mutual demonstration of love and the sharing of His gospel.

STUDY GUIDE

MEMORIZE: JOHN 3:16-17

"God loved the world so much that he gave his one and only Son so that whoever believes in him may not be lost, but have eternal life. God did not send his Son into the world to judge the world guilty, but to save the world through him.

Re-read the opening quote at the beginning of this chapter. Dissect the quote: In what ways did Jesus demonstrate His love and how did that enable Him to lead?

Write three things you have learned about Jesus:

Read Genesis 3:1-15 and explain why this event made it necessary for Jesus to be our Savior?

How did Jesus' sacrifice result in your salvation?

Why is the name of Jesus Christ so important?

SHORT ESSAY:

Directions: Answer the following essay question in at least two well-thought out paragraphs. Use at least three specific scriptures from your lesson to support your essay.

Question: Explain why the resurrection of Jesus is so important to your faith and how can you be certain of it?

LIFE APPLICATION:

Watch this video and discuss it with your Youth Pastor and friends. https://www.youtube.com/watch?v=i-PtE1BrqKU Life In 6 Words - The GOSPEL (Propaganda) [Dare 2 Share] - Weapons of Hope)

FELLOWSHIP

"Our society is filled with runaways, dropouts, and quitters. The epidemic of walking away has hit our land with effects as devastating as the bubonic plague and it has destroyed millions of effective lives and relationships. We are so self-centered that we have ceased to lay down our lives for others. We have seen others faint or walk away and we have followed in their weakness. We have fainted when we could have persevered by exchanging our strength for His! With His strength, not only could we have kept on walking, we could have run"
– Kay Arthur

FELLOWSHIP with the KING

Kay Arthur's quote speaks to our need to be in close community with God and how we have failed to respond to the needs of our neighbor. There are two aspects of fellowship that we need to understand. The first is fellowship with God. Fellowship with God is what was jeopardized when Adam and Eve sinned in the Garden of Eden. They had the joy of perfect, unblemished fellowship with God (Gen. 3:8a) but through their disobedience this perfect fellowship was lost. God desires to have a *relationship* with us. So many Christians think that all God desires from us is weekly attendance at the local church. God is a relational being. He is our

Father (2 Cor. 6:18), and no matter how good or bad your earthly father may be or has been, he can't compare to our heavenly Father whose love knows no end. Paul says in Romans 8:37-39, "Yet in all these things we are more than conquerors through Him who loved us. For I am persuaded that neither death nor life, nor angels nor principalities nor powers, nor things present nor things to come, nor height nor depth, nor any other created thing, shall be able to separate us from the love of God which is in Christ Jesus our Lord."

Your *relationship* with God is the single biggest factor in determining your consistency as a believer. Some ways that you fellowship with God are by reading His Word (the Bible), praying to Him and listening for His voice, and by doing what He's asked you to do. As with any relationship, there are two important truths we need to remember – this takes time to develop and it requires communication. Think of your relationship with your best friend– did you tell them all of your deepest fears or secrets right up front? How long did it take for you to feel comfortable with them? The psalmist writes, in Psalm 66:19-20, "But certainly God has heard me; He has attended to the voice of my prayer. Blessed be God, Who has not turned away my prayer, Nor His mercy from me." In order to have fellowship with God, who doesn't physically live near us, we have to *abide* in Him. To abide means to dwell, remain or continue. Jesus said, "Abide in Me, and I in you. As the branch cannot bear fruit of itself, unless it abides in the vine, neither can you, unless you abide in Me....You are My friends if you do whatever I command you. [15] No longer do I call you servants, for a servant does not know what his master is doing; but I have called you friends, for all things that I heard from My Father I have made known to you." (John 15:4, 14-15) If we continue to be obedient to the things Christ has *already* spoken and continue to seek (ask) Him and do what He desires for us to do on a daily basis, then our fellowship with Him will remain strong.

FELLOWSHIP about the KING

The second aspect of fellowship is fellowship with other believers. We as Christians need each other. The need for fellowship and discipleship *after* accepting Christ as your Savior has never been greater. Hopefully, we will understand this and begin to be more intentional with our discipleship methods. Most Christians will not become ministers, preachers, pastors, deacons or whatever title may be attributed to a select group of people. Every Christian, however, has the same responsibility: to share the love of Christ and ultimately to share the Gospel with others. Paul uses the word ambassador to give us a better understanding of this calling. 2 Corinthians 5:19-20 reads, "that is, that God was in Christ reconciling the world to Himself, not imputing their trespasses to them, and has committed to us the word of reconciliation. Now then, we are ambassadors for Christ, as though God were pleading through us: we implore *you* on Christ's behalf, be reconciled to God." An ambassador never speaks their own opinion, but only that of the King or country to which they belong. This means we need to know what the message of our King, Jesus Christ, is and how to convey it. One way that we learn this is by fellowshipping with other believers as was done when the church first started, "And they continued steadfastly in the apostles' doctrine and fellowship, in the breaking of bread, and in prayers (Acts 2:42)."

Church is a great place to fellowship with other believers. We gain encouragement, understanding, and our faith is increased as we talk to other believers and hear their testimonies. One of the highest praises Paul ever gave a church was to the church in Rome. Romans 1:8 says "First, I want to say that I thank my God through Jesus Christ for all of you, because people everywhere in the world are talking about your faith." The church in Rome was known for their faith. In order to be known for your faith you have to demonstrate your faith. Any church that can be unified enough to demonstrate their faith and belief in Christ is definitely a testimony to God's grace and presence. The goal of any ministry should be to bring glory to God. The 12 disciples asked Jesus how people would know they were His disciples; Jesus said, "by the love you have for each other. (John 13:35)"

To have a reputation of loving each other and not one of bickering and forming cliques would be an incredible testimony to the world.

Hebrews 10:25 says "Forsaking not the assembly of the saints." Some may say that once you're saved, you don't really need to come to church or that it's not a big deal to belong to a church or a church ministry. Although church attendance is not going to determine your salvation, it's very important because fellowship cannot be attained on our own. Your church should be a place where people come together as men and women of God and celebrate what we've done as Christians for the kingdom throughout the week. The work of being a Christian is done Monday through Saturday, so when we come together on Sunday (or any other day), we come together to fellowship, to enjoy and celebrate God and to receive encouragement to go out to do more of what we've been called to do in the first place. It's important to come together with other believers so that we can strengthen each other. We can't make it through this Christian walk alone and we need encouragement from time to time. We also need to be challenged to grow. In 1 Samuel 30:6 it says that David encouraged himself in the Lord but he was still hanging out with other believers. Through shared fellowship and community, we grow as Christians. When we come together we should stir up love and exhort (which means to urge or to advise or caution earnestly) one another in our faith (Hebrews 10:24).

FELLOWSHIP in the KINGDOM

What's the benefit of being around other Christians? What can the church do for your life? What can you do for the church? Daniel 4:3, Romans 14:7 14:10 and 14:17 show us that we have to stand together because, just like there is a Kingdom of God, there is also a kingdom of darkness. A Kingdom is a territory, governed by a King where the influence of his will and intent are clear. The kingdom produces citizens that reflect the morality, nature and culture of the king. When we get saved we become citizens of the Kingdom of God. Once we are there we need to be discipled (taught) how to reflect the nature, morality and culture of our King (Jesus Christ).

We can't expect people to turn into disciples just because they come to church or a youth meeting. In the 'great commission' Jesus said to *make* disciples (Matthew 28:19-20) and the only method He gives us for accomplishing that mission is to teach them. It is our responsibility as Christians to make sure that unity, faith, fellowship and an understanding of the word are paramount in our lives and our ministries.

STUDY GUIDE

MEMORIZE: HEBREWS 10:25
"Forsaking not the assembly of the saints."

Re-read the opening quote at the beginning of this chapter. Dissect the quote: What happens when people feel alone due to lack of fellowship?

In what ways do you fellowship? List three ways:

1.

2.

3.

SHORT ANSWER:
1. Why is fellowship with God so important?

2. What can cause you to lose your fellowship with God?

3. Read Romans 14:7-10 and explain how that passage relates to fellowship?

4. What are we supposed to reflect as citizens of the Kingdom of God?

LIFE APPLICATION:
Look at the people you hang with. Look at who your friends are. Do you share the same goals? Do you even know what their goals and desires are? Do you share the same faith? If you don't already have them, take some time this month and find some people who believe what you believe and have goals in life like you do. They don't have to have the same goal but they do have to believe they have a purpose. Then make a point of spending time with these purpose-filled individuals at least once a week.

"Grace is the pleasure of God to magnify the worth of God by giving sinners the right and power to delight in God without obscuring the glory of God." – John Piper

One of the topics that Paul dealt with in great detail throughout the course of his ministry and in all of his epistles (letters) was grace. Grace is a church word that gets thrown around a lot, but few have a firm understanding of what it is. Grace is God's gift to us. Grace is *getting from God what you don't deserve.* Do not confuse grace with mercy – which is *not getting from God what you do deserve.*

His GRACE gave LIFE

Romans 5:8 states that, "But God demonstrates His own love toward us in that while we were still sinners, Christ died for us." We need to remember that grace is a gift that has been given to us. We are sinners and God sees that we often make bad decisions. In His grace, He sent His Son to die for us, so that we wouldn't have to die and be separated from Him for eternity. Through this sacrifice, we can have eternal life with God through Jesus. One pastor put it this way: "Grace was in heaven and chose to come to earth in human form so that He could die and defeat death to give us access to God and to heaven if we chose Him (Jesus)." Sometimes we can receive grace and not fully understand or comprehend the impact it has on our lives. There was a man who had always dreamed of going on a Caribbean cruise, but knew that he could never afford such a luxurious vacation. A close friend heard about his desire and decided to bless him with the cruise. The man was ecstatic and asked what was included with the cruise. His friend shared that it included the flight to the cruise ship and the seven-day cruise. The man was excited, but did not have enough money for food, so he decided to pack food for seven days for his trip. As he enjoyed the free Caribbean cruise, he would walk by all the buffets and restaurants each day and head to his cabin to eat the food he had packed. On the fourth day of the cruise he decided to ask one of the cruise staff how much the buffet cost for one meal. The staff looked surprised and said "Sir you don't have to pay anything. The buffets, restaurants and snack shops are included with your cruise ticket. Eat all you want!" What the man had not understood was that his ticket entitled him to everything.

A lot of Christians are like this. They are limiting themselves to the things of this world and do not understand grace and what it means to their life. Most Christians define it as God's unmerited, or undeserved, favor toward sinners (which is true). However, we cannot forget that grace is also the inexhaustible supply of God's goodness whereby He does for us what we cannot do for ourselves. This doesn't mean that God will give you all the money, houses, cars and clothes that you want but it does mean He will love you unconditionally and take care of you as a gracious father.

His GRACE shows LOVE

The New Testament was originally written in Greek. The Greek language has several words for love – 'Philia' which is brotherly love, 'eros' which is erotic love, and 'agape' which is unconditional, self-sacrificing, active, unyielding, and thoughtful love. This unconditional love is rarely displayed among humans, but it is God's specialty. John 14:21 says, "He who has My commandments and keeps them, it is he who loves Me. And he who loves Me will be loved by My Father, and I will love him and manifest Myself to him." John 15:12-13 says, "This is My commandment, that you love one another as I have loved you. Greater love has no one than this, than to lay down one's life for his friends." Think for a minute about the people in your life. Who would you honestly be willing to die for? Thankfully, you don't have to make that decision. Romans 5:7-8 says, " For scarcely for a righteous man will one die; yet perhaps for a good man someone would even dare to die. [8] But God demonstrates His own love toward us, in that while we were still sinners, Christ died for us."

Even if we made that sacrifice it would be imperfect and save no one. We have to remember that Jesus lived his earthly life for more than 30 years without sinning just to save each one of us. Some of us can't go a day without having an impure thought, cursing, fighting, being disobedient or doing anything that would offend a holy and righteous God. Christ knew that you and I would never be deserving of His grace and favor but He chose to give it to us anyway because even before you loved Him, He loved you. Wow! We need to do our best to extend the same kind of love and grace to those we encounter every day.

STUDY GUIDE

MEMORIZE: EPHESIANS 2:8-9

"I mean that you have been saved by grace through believing. You did not save yourselves; it was a gift from God. It was not the result of your own efforts, so you cannot brag about it."

Re-read the opening quote at the beginning of this chapter. Dissect the quote: How does God's grace bring Him pleasure?

ACTION:
List three "Acts of Service" you will complete:
1.

2.

3.

SHORT ANSWER:
1) How did God demonstrate His love for us?

2) Why is John 15:12-13 so significant?

3) Why don't you deserve God's grace?

4) In what ways can we share the grace and love of God?

LIFE APPLICATION:
This week fulfill three "Acts of Service." Some examples:

- Get a couple of friends to clean a parking lot or school sports field
- Volunteer at a retirement home
- Volunteer at a homeless shelter or food pantry

"Prayer is as natural an expression of faith as breathing is of life"
– Jonathan Edwards

*"*To be a Christian without prayer is no more possible
than to be alive without breathing.*"*
- Dr. Martin Luther King

The REASON for PRAYER

Think about your relationship with your best friend or someone
that you have known for a long time. Ask yourself how you know
so much about them and they about you? The answer is communication. You don't get to know one another by talking just once or
twice, but by having consistent and unending communication - that
teaches you about that person, as they learn about you as well. It is
easier to talk to them as the days, weeks, months and years go by.
In fact, it is impossible to have a close relationship without good
communication. Good communication also leads to greater trust,
accountability, and understanding.

Just as communication enables us to build relationships with
other people, communication is necessary for you to build a
relationship with God.   Your communication with God is con-

tingent on your prayer; it is your lifeline to God. We will get to know Him better and He will get to know us and respond to us accordingly. As men and women of God, it is our responsibility to pray. The results will be just the same as what we experience when we have good communication with our friends and family.

The ROUTINE for PRAYER

There is an acronym we can use while praying: ACTS. Use this tool as you pray. The first letter 'A' stands for *adoration*. With any prayer we should always start by giving God the glory He deserves before we ask for anything. Begin by praising God and telling Him how awesome and how magnificent He is. Tell Him He's holy (Lev. 11:45), righteous (Psalm 45:6), and perfect (Deut. 32:4). Tell Him that He's never made a mistake (Psalm 18:30) and that you love Him. Thank Him for loving you (Romans 8:35-39). Tell Him that you trust Him (2 Samuel 22:3) without a shadow of a doubt. Just begin by adoring Him and speaking loving words of admiration before you ask for anything for yourself. Tell Him that you respect Him and respect His position and come humbly to His throne by way of Jesus Christ (Hebrews 4:16). This part of prayer is so important because it puts things in proper perspective. Although God knows He's holy, righteous, perfect and powerful, He loves to hear His children say it. He's been waiting for you to speak to Him and to speak well of Him (Psalm 102:18). This is our opportunity to say thank you and to give Him what we owe Him.

Once the stage is set and we have God's attention we need to make sure that we are cleansed before we ask for anything. To do this we confess (acknowledge or admit) our sins – the 'C' is for *confession*. Read 1 John 1:8-10. It shows us that we have to be honest about our sin. Most of the time, we know when we've done wrong. Therefore, when we confess our sins to God we need to be specific. He already knows what you've done, but He wants to hear you say it. The good news is that "If we **confess** our **sins**, He is faithful and just to forgive us our **sins** and to cleanse us from all unrighteousness." (1 John 1:9) Confess your sins to Him and allow Him to cleanse you before you make any requests. Don't let sin hinder your prayers. Also, specific prayers are accurate and focused (James 5:16). In other words, these are prayers that you know will be heard. As you develop a prayer life and learn to pray the Word of God back to God, you can be confident that He will hear and answer your prayers because He is faithful to His word. You will develop a greater relationship with God, your Father. As with any good relationship, communication has to be a two-way street. Prayer is simply talking to God. God will speak to us while we are in prayer or when we read the Bible. Sometimes He will answer through other people. However, His decision of when and how to respond is up to Him, but our responsibility remains the same.

The "T" stands for *thanksgiving*. We need to thank Him for everything He's done for us and everything He has been to us. We can even thank Him for everything He's going to do, because we have faith that He will do everything that we ask in the name of Jesus Christ if it's in His will (John 14:13-14). Also, we believe and trust that He sees us and He hears us (1 John 5:14-15). He's worthy of praise and we should be thankful just to be loved by Him and to be known by Him. Be thankful to be adored by Him. Be thankful that He saved you. Be thankful that He got you out of the hands of the enemy (the devil). Be thankful that He protected you from the lasting effects of the sinful lifestyle that you were involved in or are involved in. We give Him thanks before we ask for anything, because whether or not He answers our prayer the way we want Him to answer it, He's still worthy and deserving of thanks. He's still deserving of our gratitude just for sending His Son to die for us. Thank Him for covering us in the blood of Jesus, which Christ shed on the cross. The blood that He shed is what allows God to look upon us and dwell in and with us. It's because of that blood that He no longer sees our imperfect lives covered in sin, but He only sees the blood of His perfect Son. Thank Him for hiding and throwing away our sins and for remembering them no more (Psalm 103:12).

The 'S' stands for *supplication*, which means petition, request or plea. This is where we begin to make our requests known and where we begin to ask for what we need from God. Once again, be specific. Get away from prayers such as "God I pray that you bless my whole family" and replace them with prayers such as, "God I pray that you bless my mother and help her get the job that she is interviewing for tomorrow" or "heal my aunt Teresa, who is in the hospital, suffering with lung cancer." When we are in the store and want something we have no problem being very specific! We need to be just as specific to God and speak to Him as our father, because He *is* our Father. In fact, He is a perfect and holy Father and wants to take care of us the way any good father should (2 Cor. 6:18). He's not a ghost or a cloud in the sky. He is a living entity and He is our Father; we should address Him as such.

Here is an example of a prayer: "Father I adore You, I give You the glory for who You are. I confess that I've sinned (and then be specific in what way you've sinned.) I thank You for everything that You've done, everything You are, everything You've been to me, and I need You to please help me. I've already studied with the desire to get an A on this test, but I still need your help, and I pray that you will bring all things to my remembrance and give me peace during my test. In Jesus' name I pray, amen."

The RESPONSE to our PRAYER

Your prayers are precious to God and He takes them very seriously. In Revelation 5:8 and in Revelation 8:3, the scene portrayed is the angels delivering the prayers of the saints (Christians) in golden bowls. Imagine that. Our prayers are so precious that they're hand-delivered to Jesus in a golden bowl of incense. He individually takes time to hear each request and deal with them accordingly. He takes time to answer those prayers and to intercede on our behalf with the Father. Jesus is able to intercede for us in heaven because He lived as a man, and knows how difficult it is for us to walk the way we've been called to walk and for us to live a life of purity. Psalms 102:17 says, "He regards the prayer of the destitute and does not despise their prayer." In other words, He doesn't just push the prayers away as insignificant. It is important for us to understand that our prayers *are* significant. They are significant in the body of Christ and in the Kingdom of God and we play an important role in both facets.

In Matthew 6:5-13, Jesus teaches the disciples to pray and it's important for us to read this and to learn it. In fact it's one of the only instances where the disciples asked Jesus to teach them something specific. They must have known and been able to see from watching Jesus that prayer was communication with God and was vitally important. It's important for our prayers to be specific and honest. Our prayers should not be prayed to receive acclaim from others, or to show off. We should pray because it is literally communicating with God. This is how we talk to Him and how He hears us. When possible, it is ideal to pray out loud. When we make known our requests and we put them out there in the spirit realm, especially if others are there to hear, we demonstrate faith that God will act. He is faithful and God will not be mocked (Gal. 6:7). When we come to Him with that type of confidence, especially by praying His Word back to Him, He will respond (Hebrews 10:23). God is not a man that He should lie (Numbers 23:19).

1 Thessalonians 5:17 says to pray without ceasing. That doesn't mean we're always walking around praying out loud, but as we get more used to praying we will be able to pray while we're walking and even while we're talking with someone. We will be able to pray silently in our minds. In addition to our prayers, the Holy Spirit makes intercession (the act of pleading on somebody's behalf) for us and prays when we can't pray (Romans 8:26-27) or don't know what to pray for. If you have trouble thinking of what to pray for, remember that one of the strongest prayers you can pray is praying God's word back to Him. That's why it's so important to know and seek to be educated in the Word of God.

STUDY GUIDE

MEMORIZE: JAMES 5:16

"Confess your trespasses to one another, and pray for one another, that you may be healed. The effective, fervent prayer of a righteous man avails much."

Re-read the opening quote at the beginning of this chapter. Dissect the quote: How is prayer connected to faith?

ACTION STEP 1

Spend fifteen minutes in prayer every morning this week. In your prayers pray for people and things other than yourself. Examples: Pray for missionaries in countries where Christianity is prohibited. Pray for those whom you know that have rejected Jesus. Pray for the hurt that is in this world (natural disaster, disease, hunger, etc.)

Teach them how to pray (ACTS):

Fill in the blanks:

_____ – Give God the glory He deserves before you ask for anything

_____ – Confess your sins to Him and allow Him to cleanse you before you make your request. Sin can hinder your prayers. Be honest in your confession.

_____ – Thank Him for everything He's done for you and everything He's been to you.

_____ – This is where you make your request known to Him

READ: MATTHEW 6:5-13
Jesus teaches the disciples to _____
List 5 things Jesus instructs us to pray for:

Think about an area of your life that you struggle in. (i.e. lust, lying) List 3 scriptures that deal with that issue. Post them on your bathroom mirror or next to your bed and pray those scriptures every day for a month.

1.

2.

3.

LIFE APPLICATION:

Take action! Find a public place that seems to be a trouble spot in the community. (Take a friend with you if it's safer.) Go to that place (i.e. a park, the mall, a school, etc.) and pray in or around that area for God to change things for the better and to allow His Kingdom to advance in that area. Be consistent and see what God does or leads you to do. You can also do the same activity in your own house if you feel things need to change there as well.

THE BIBLE

"Moreover, the ability of Jesus to recall so freely Old Testament passages must have impressed the disciples with the necessity of learning the Scriptures by heart, and letting them become the authority for their pronouncements. In everything it was made abundantly clear that the word written in the Scriptures and the word spoken by Christ were not in contradiction, but rather complemented each other. That which Jesus taught was also to be cherished by His disciples. Hence, the Scriptures, coupled with His own utterance, became for them the objective basis of their faith in Christ." – Robert E. Coleman

In the middle ages, soldiers would move out to battle and would equip themselves with body armor to protect them from attacks, seen and unseen. In order to win the battle and to achieve victory, they needed a tool or a weapon that could cut through the opposing forces. As men and women of God that weapon for us is the Word of God. Nothing is more essential than equipping ourselves with the Word and then to speak and pray that Word in times of desperation, as well as in times of joy. We get to know our Lord and our power by knowing the Word of God. It and it alone is the truth that we rely upon.

The PURPOSE of the Word

The Word of God exists for our instruction, guidance and knowledge about the will of God and is our source of information about the God we serve (2 Tim. 3:16). There are two major parts to the Bible, also known as the Word of God: the Old Testament and the New Testament. The 39 books of the Old Testament give us the history of humanity and specifically the children of Israel. Moses wrote the first five books of the Bible also known as the Pentateuch (Genesis, Exodus, Leviticus, Numbers, and Deuteronomy). These five books give us the account of creation, the story of Noah and the ark, Moses leading the Hebrew slaves to freedom away from the Pharaoh of Egypt and eventually into the Promised Land. The Old Testament provides us with more than 300 prophecies about the birth, life, ministry, kingdom, death, and resurrection of the coming Messiah or Savior. God spoke through men and prophets to let them know what to tell the children of Israel about how to live. For example, Deuteronomy 6:4-7 reads, "Hear, O Israel: The Lord our God, the Lord is one. You shall love the Lord your God with all your heart and with all your soul and with all your might. And these words that I command you today shall be on your heart. You shall teach them diligently to your children, and shall talk of them when you sit in your house, and when you walk by the way, and when you lie down, and when you rise."

God also gave us insight on what to look for regarding "the Seed" (Jesus Christ). He would be sent from heaven and into the virgin, Mary, and would grow to be the Savior of the world. Isaiah 9:6-7 reads, "For to us a child is born, to us a son is given; and the government shall be upon his shoulder, and his name shall be called Wonderful Counselor, Mighty God, Everlasting Father, Prince of Peace. Of the increase of His government and of peace there will be no end, on the throne of David and over His kingdom, to establish it and to uphold it with justice and with righteousness from this time forth and forevermore. The zeal of the Lord of hosts will do this."

The New Testament has 27 books and begins with the fulfillment of this and many other similar prophecies. The first four books of the New Testament (Matthew, Mark, Luke and John) are called the gospels. Gospel means "good news." Matthew, Mark and Luke are known as synoptic gospels because they record similar accounts of the birth, life, ministry, death, and resurrection of Jesus Christ. The same accounts of what took place can often be found in all three. John wrote his gospel much later. Because the life of Jesus Christ was already well documented, John dealt more with the deity (Godly characteristics) of Christ and he gave us some insights about Christ that weren't as commonly known and that needed to be recorded. John, like several of the other gospel writers, lets us know that he was an eyewitness to what Jesus did and who He was. They were not guessing or making assumptions about what they heard someone else say (2 Peter 1:16-21).

We can rest assured that Christ was born, lived a sinless life as the Son of God, died for our sins and that God raised Him from the grave three days after He was crucified on the cross. John writes in John 21:24-25 "This is the disciple who testifies of these things, and wrote these things; and we know that his testimony is true. And there are also many other things that Jesus did, which if they were written one by one, I suppose that even the world itself could not contain the books that would be written." He also lets us know the purpose for why he wrote the epistles (letters) in 1 John 5:12-13, "Whoever has the Son has life; whoever does not have the Son of God does not have life. I write these things to you who believe in the name of the Son of God that you may know that you have eternal life." One of the most prolific writers of the New Testament was Paul. Of the 27 books that make up the New Testament, the apostle Paul wrote 13 of them: Romans, 1 & 2 Corinthians, Galatians, Ephesians, Philippians, Colossians, 1 & 2 Thessalonians, 1 & 2 Timothy, Titus, and Philemon. His revelation gives us much insight on how to live a Christ-like lifestyle as well as how to bring others into the Kingdom of God and disciple them so that they remain effective citizens of the Kingdom.

Testament means covenant or agreement. The New Testament dictates God's desire to have relationship with us and instructs us not to sin our way into hell, which is eternal separation from God. It also informs us that there is another way the story of our lives can end and that way was paved by the sacrifice Jesus Christ paid on the cross. Peter said in Acts 4:11-12, "This Jesus is the stone that was rejected by you, the builders, which has become the cornerstone. And there is salvation in no one else, for there is no other name under heaven given among men by which we must be saved." Once we understand the purpose of the Word, we can begin to realize the power of the Word and how to live life as a citizen of the Kingdom of God.

The POSITION of the Word

The Word of God, the Bible, is our basic instructions before leaving earth. The Word is what sustains us as Christians. Here is another way to think about it and understand the importance of the Bible in our lives. If you don't eat food every day you won't operate at full capacity and if you don't eat for long enough you will die. Spiritually, the word of God is what we need to feed ourselves. We will be unable to sustain the life and lifestyle God wants for us to live if we continue to starve ourselves spiritually. 1 Peter 1:25- 2:2 says "but the word of the Lord remains forever and this word is the good news that was preached to you, so put away all malice and all deceit and hypocrisy and envy and all slander. Like newborn infants long for the pure spiritual milk that by it you may grow up into salvation." In the same way babies begin by drinking milk and then move on to solid food we need to mature from milk to solid food (1 Cor. 3:1-2). In other words we need to begin with the foundational concepts outlined in these pages and build upon them so that we grow spiritually. Paul says in 2 Timothy 2:15 "study to show yourself approved'. This applies to each individual Christian and every man and woman of God. It doesn't matter whether you're a pastor, preacher, minister or even if you don't consider yourself to be anyone special. Everyone has the responsibility to study the Word of God for their own sake, and for the sake of their family both now and in the future. You should find ways to study the Word on your own. Some people write Bible verses on index cards and try and memorize them like flash cards. Some people pick a person from the Bible that they feel they can relate to and study all that the Bible says about them. For example, you could study David or

Paul or Peter. You could also study a topic such as peace, grace, faith, or love and see what the Word says about that topic. Attending a church or a youth group doesn't guarantee your spirit will be fed either. Coming together is great, but coming together and not eating is a shame. God deserves first position in our lives. If we seek Him, His Kingdom and His righteousness first, we will have everything that we need (Matthew 6:33). Righteousness is adherence to God's standards and commandments. In other words it's being right based on *His* rules.

One of the main ways that we seek Him is by reading the Word He has laid out for us. Joshua 1:8 says, "This Book of the Law shall not depart from your mouth, but you shall meditate on it day and night, so that you may be careful to do according to all that is written in it. For then you will make your way prosperous, and then you will have good success." In this passage, meditate does not mean sitting with your legs crossed and humming. It does mean to read the word and think about it throughout the busy days that we live. It also gives us power to succeed and be prosperous. The most awesome thing about it is that the power is at our disposal if we read, trust and believe the Word. The scripture says, "*you* will make your way prosperous and *you* will have good success." Wow! The Word has to have the top *position* in our lives.

The POWER of the Word

If the Word is first in our lives and if it is the first place we turn to before we make the mistake of taking matters into our own hands; we will experience the *power* of His Word. Hebrews 4:12 reads, "For the Word of God is living and active, sharper than any two-edged sword, piercing to the division of soul and of spirit, of joints and of marrow, and discerning the thoughts and intentions of the heart." This means that if we look for validation or verification, which is proof regarding any issue or topic in the Word of God, it will give us precise answers. Sometimes His Word will cut through the façade (cover-up or disguise) that we sometimes put up and will get to the root of our issue or concern. In other words, we can't hide from the truth that the Word will reveal to us and about us.

When a sharp sword slices through something it is a clean cut. There are no jagged edges. When the Word of God penetrates our thoughts, heart, soul and mind some things will be cut away completely to make us who He wants us to be. Think of God and His Word as a precise surgeon. If we had a tumor, we would a want a surgeon with a steady hand to use his or her scalpel to remove it. We may not like the process, but in the end we would be grateful to the surgeon for saving our life (Hebrews 12:5-8). The Word of God operates the same way. We may not like the process of renewal or regeneration (to restore or be reborn), but we will thank Him in the end. The Word of God will either affirm (to cosign) or negate (to cancel out or go against) what we say or do. We need to use the Word as our guide and as our proof test for the truth. The word will decipher or make sense of everything including the intentions of people we come in contact with.

The Word of God will give us the clear-cut answer to every issue, incident, or situation that we could ever encounter. There's nothing new under the sun (Ecclesiastes 1:9). The Word has already dealt with everything. We just have to read the book (the Bible) to find the answer for that specific thing. The Word deals with everything from how to handle an offense from your brother (Matthew 18:15-17) to your responsibility to pay for taxes (Mark 12:14-17). The Word is designed as a sword and Paul describes it in such a way that it is something that will cut you and convict you of all unrighteousness. Conviction is a beautiful thing for a man or woman of God to have. It means that we understand and acknowledge our sin and have a desire to do something about it and prevent ourselves from sinning that way ever again.

The Word helps us do that but the Word also brings us into correction, "All Scripture is breathed out by God and profitable for teaching, for reproof (conviction), for correction, and for training in righteousness, that the man of God may be competent, equipped for every good work." (2 Timothy 3:16). It brings us into a deeper relationship with God through Christ. We can thank God for giving us the Bible, which is our blueprint for life. It is the instructions for what to do, how to do it, how to live and how to conduct ourselves to best represent His Kingdom on earth.

In Ephesians 6:17b, Paul lets us know that the sword is the Word of the Spirit and it's what we fight with! In that whole chapter of Ephesians 6, he's detailing the armor of God and the only offensive or attack weapon that we've been given is the Word of God. This is the only thing we can use to combat the enemy. Everything else is for defense. The shield and the helmet are present to block the assault that the enemy launches at us through words, through thoughts, through temptation, through different situations and scenarios, but the way that we attack and defeat him is with the Word of God. The word does not return void ("So shall my word be that goes out from my mouth; it shall not return to me void (empty), but it shall accomplish that which I purpose, and shall succeed in the thing for which I sent it." Isaiah 55:11). This means that the word is always successful at what it is sent to accomplish! The right word spoken in the right situation can save us from going in the wrong direction. The Word is what we fight with – by speaking it in and against ungodly thoughts, temptations, trials and difficult situations.

We can't use the Word of God to fight if we don't know the Word of God. Therefore, we need to begin to learn how to get in the Word and study the Word. We should find truths and revelations that we can pull out that will help to make us better and sharper. We should find specific scriptures that deal with issues that we have admitted to. When we go through those situations or when those thoughts come in our minds, we can speak and pray the scripture immediately because it's already in our mind. As we begin to develop a mental registry for scriptures as if we had a Biblical "google" in our brain, we will be able to pull them up at a moment's notice. However, you can't remember something you've never heard. The Holy Spirit, who brings all things to our remembrance (Rom. 8:26-27), will actually speak on our behalf, even if we find ourselves in a situation where we don't know the right words to offer to God in prayer. The Holy Spirit fights for us and *with* us to give us the victory that we need and deserve. It is true that God desires for us to store His Word in our hearts so that it becomes our defense and shield against the enemy; yet, God's power, through the work of the Holy Spirit in us, is so strong that our moans and groans become words that God understands. Think about it like this, the Holy Spirit knows the Word of God and wants the best for you but you have to want the best for yourself and be willing to put in the time and effort to learn God's Word and to learn what pleases Him. Once this occurs then you can begin to pray in line with the Holy Spirit so that you accomplish the will of God for your life. For example, when you are challenged for your faith at school you can pray 1 Peter 3:15-16 which says, "But sanctify the Lord God in your hearts, and always *be* ready to *give* a defense to everyone who asks you a reason for the hope that is in you, with meekness and fear; [16] having a good conscience, that when they defame you as evildoers, those who revile your good conduct in Christ may be ashamed."

The PRESENCE of the Word

In John 6:63, Jesus instructs us that "It is the Spirit who gives life; the flesh is no help at all. The words that I have spoken to you are spirit and life." His words are alive and keep you and your spirit alive. There are two words for life in the Greek, one is "psuche" and the other is "zoe". "Psuche" is the soul or the breath of life. We would probably consider this the more spiritual of the two words if someone just brought these two words to us. "Zoe" means active or adamant and alive. The word that Jesus uses is "zoe", which means alive. He doesn't use the word that sounds more spiritual, but He is teaching us that the words He speaks and the words that we speak are literally living and that the Word of God is literally alive and active when we speak it. Spiritually speaking, the Word takes legs and walks. Don't get scared. This simply means that it has the ability and authority to do things on the earth that will benefit and bless our lives and the lives of those around us. The presence of the Word in our lives is therefore the only way we can move things from the spiritual realm and experience them in the natural realm. In other words, if we want God to do something for us, we need to be on one accord with what He has *already* spoken and promised.

Psalm 119 is the longest psalm in the Bible, but it deals entirely with the Word of God - the importance of the Word, the Joy of the Word, what the Word does for us, where the Word comes from, how the Word blesses us and how the Word benefits and blesses others.

Psalm 119:11 says, "I have hidden your Word in my heart, that I might not sin against you." This indicates that if the word is in us it will help keep us from sinning. We need to have His Word hidden in our hearts so that when we think certain thoughts that aren't of God, the Word immediately will pop into our minds. This can happen only if we've trained our minds and our memory is triggered to recall scripture as opposed to going to another place of engaging in sin. The presence of the Word brings a power to live a God-pleasing life unlike any self-help book that could ever be compiled. It is the foundation on which God wants and needs for us to stand firmly.

STUDY GUIDE

MEMORIZE: HEBREWS 4:12

"For the Word of God is living and active, sharper than any two-edged sword, piercing to the division of soul and of spirit, of joints and of marrow, and discerning the thoughts and intentions of the heart."

Re-read the opening quote at the beginning of this chapter. Dissect the quote: What did the disciples learn from Jesus' knowledge of the scriptures?

SHORT ANSWER

Directions: Answer each of the following questions in at least TWO COMPLETE sentences. The answers come from your lesson.

1. What are some characteristics of the Old Testament books?

2. What is the purpose for the 4 gospels?

3. 2 Tim. 2:15 says to *study* to show *yourself* approved. Why is this important?

4. Explain Ephesians 6:17 and how it relates to our victory over the enemy?

5. What does Jesus' statement in John 6:63 tell you about the Word of God?

6. What does Psalm 119 deal with?

7. Read Psalm 119 this week and write 3 verses from Psalm 119 that bless you.

a)

b)

c)

LIFE APPLICATION:
There is a causal link to our ability to please God and our time spent in the Word.

Hebrews 11:1 states, "Faith means being sure of the things we hope for and knowing that something is real even if we do not see it."

Hebrews 11:6a states, "Without faith no one can please God."

Romans 10:17 states, "So then faith *comes* by hearing, and hearing by the word of God."

If you ask anyone they would most likely tell you that they desire to please God. However, in order to please God you need faith (Hebrews 11:6a). The way you get or increase your faith is by being in (studying) the Word of God (Romans 10:17). Therefore, not studying makes it very difficult to get the faith that is required in order to please God.

CONCLUSION

"According to the grace of God which was given to me, as a wise master builder I have laid the foundation, and another builds on it. But let each one take heed how he builds it. For no other foundation can anyone lay than that which is laid, which is Jesus Christ."– 1 Corinthians 3:10-11 NKJV

Now that you've gone through this course, you have had the opportunity to impart the foundation of our belief in Christ as our Savior to our young people. A house without a solid foundation will not stand. Likewise, a person's faith built on shaky or questionable teachings will not stand against the attack of the enemy or the trials of life. There are certain *truths* that Christianity is built upon and those are based on the life and words of Jesus Christ and God's work through prophets and other mighty men and women of God since the beginning of time until years after Christ's departure back to heaven. All of these *truths* are recorded in the Bible – our foundation as Christians. It is the complete, authentic, veritable and prophetic Word of God.

It is my hope that within this course, the road to salvation and the need for salvation will become clear. Evidence has been presented to assure our young people that God has made a way out of temptation, provided tools for living a Christian lifestyle and has paved the way for their eventual entrance into heaven. Through an understanding of forgiveness, they will experience a new beginning as a confident man or woman of God. As they've studied and meditated on the Word, they will learn the nature of God the Father, Son, and Holy Spirit as well as that of our collective adversary, the devil. Then through fellowship and discipleship and exercising their God-given power as members of the body of Christ they will now be able to fight the good fight and finish *their* race being able to say, "I have kept the faith."

What will occur as a result of this course is an emergence of young men and women of God who will intentionally live a life that is pleasing to God. Having a strong foundation will allow them to grow into mature Christians, unwavering in their faith and able to conduct themselves as living epistles wherever they go and in whatever they do. God is faithful and He says that if we train up a child in the way he should go, when they are old they will not depart from it. This course allows us to put God to the test and it will foster a long lasting testament to His glory. Eyes have not seen, and ears have not heard what young people can promulgate when they are given an accurate and solid foundation.

Bibliography

1) "Have You Heard the Good News of Salvation?" *Billy Graham Evangelistic Association*. 27 July 2010. Web. accessed 19 Aug. 2013. <http://billygraham.org/story/have-you-heard-the-good-news-of-salvation/>.

2) "The Power In Praise and Worship." *HubPages*. 30 Sept. 2011. Web. accessed 19 June 2013. <http://twill4jc.hubpages.com/hub/Praise-and-Worship>.

3) West, Cornell. H*ope on a Tightrope : Words and Wisdom* Carlsbad, CA: Smiley Books, 2008

4) Arthur, Kay. For Today and Tomorrow, God, How Can I Live? Eugene, OR: Harvest House Publishers, 2004

5) Piper, John. The Pleasures of God: Meditations on God's Delight in Being God by John Piper Colorado Springs, CO: WaterBrook Multnomah, Colorado Springs, 2000

6) The Works of Jonathan Edwards, A.M.: With an Essay on His Genius and Writings, Volume 2 **by** Jonathan Edwards, Henry Rogers, Sereno Edwards Dwight Publisher; W. Ball, 1839 Page 75

7) Wiersbe, Warren W. Be Determined: Standing Firm in the Face of Opposition Colorado Springs, CO: David C. Cook, 1992.

8) Coleman, Robert. The Master Plan of Evangelism. Grand Rapids, MI: Fleming H. Revell Company, Grand Rapids, MI, 1972

9) Jeffrey, Grant R. The Signature of God. Colorado Springs, CO: WaterBrook Press, 1996

10) Monroe, Myles. Kingdom Principles: Preparing for Kingdom Experience and Expansion. Shippensburg, PA: Destiny Image Publishers, Inc., 2006

THE AUTHOR

Alex McElroy is a minister at New Life Covenant Southeast Church and has been serving in youth ministry for over 10 years. He believes strongly in Jesus' example of discipleship and has discipled numerous teens and many adults. He also oversees the Education Department at New Life Covenant Southeast Church and teaches both youth and adults the foundational concepts of the Word of God as well as the principles of the Kingdom of God. Alex has begun training teachers so that they can be developed in their gifts in order to maximize their effectiveness in and for the Kingdom of God. Alex has been married to his loving and supportive wife Kasie for over 7 years and has two beautiful daughters who continue to inspire and push him to be a better man of God.

Contact Minister Alex McElroy
Phone: 312-878-7783
Min.AlexMcElroy@gmail.com
Facebook: Min Alex McElroy
Twitter: @MinAlexMcElroy